WRITTEN BY
BRIGITTE GANDIOL-COPPIN, ODILE BOMBARDE,
CORINNE COURTALON, MONIQUE COURTAULT, CLARISSE DENIAU,
MARIE FARRÉ, DOMINIQUE JOLY, CLAUDE MOATTI

COVER DESIGN BY
STEPHANIE BLUMENTHAL

TRANSLATED BY
MARY LOGUE

ADAPTED BY
ROBERT NEUMILLER

PUBLISHED BY CREATIVE EDUCATION
123 South Broad Street, Mankato, Minnesota 56001
Creative Education is an imprint of The Creative Company

Library of Congress Cataloging-in-Publication Data
[Vivre au temps jadis. English]
Ancient cultures / by Brigitte Gandiol-Coppin et al.
(Creative discoveries) Includes index.
Summary: Describes the people and their way of life in ancient times.
ISBN: 0-88682-949-6
1. Civilization, Ancient—Juvenile literature.   2. Archaeology—Juvenile literature.
3. Antiquities—Juvenile literature.   4. Civilization—History—Juvenile literature.
[1. Civilization, Ancient.   2. Archaeology.   3. Antiquities.   4. Civilization—History]
I. Bombarde, Odile.   II. Courtalon, Corinne.   III. Title.   IV. Series.
CB311.G28   1999
909—dc21   98-19978

First Edition

2 4 6 8 9 7 5 3 1

ANCIENT CIVILIZATIONS

CONTENTS

CREATIVE EDUCATION

Prehistory

Many scientists believe that humans first appeared on Earth about three million years ago. Then, about 700,000 years ago, these early humans made a discovery that changed their lives, and future lives, forever—they learned to make fire.

Early hunters

By the time the last ice age was ending, about 15,000 years ago, humans looked quite a bit like we do. From bones, archeologists have studied their lives. Early man had by then learned to shape stone, such as flint, into tools for cutting up animals or scraping hides. By studying artifacts, archeologists have learned much about how Stone Age people lived.

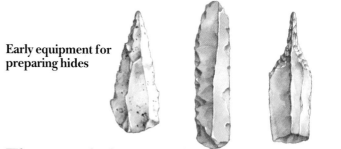

Early equipment for preparing hides

These early humans invented weapons such as lances, arrowheads, and harpoons. From pieces of bone, these people made needles to sew clothing out of the skins of the animals they hunted. People also made jewelry from shells and ivory. As the glaciers of the Ice Age receded, people settled the newly exposed land.

Life during the Stone Age

By rubbing two pieces of flint together

or by turning two pieces of dry wood

or by spinning a stick with a bow

a spark would light a fire.

People at this time were nomadic hunters and gatherers. They followed the herds of wild animals that they hunted for food, such as reindeer, bear, mammoths, and buffalo. Stone Age people also gathered fruits and wild plants and took eggs from birds' nests.

The land bridge
By this time people also began to inhabit North and South America. They arrived from Asia by crossing a land bridge, called the Bering Strait, to Alaska. This was created when sea levels dropped during the Ice Age.

Cave paintings such as this have been found in Spain and France. Early humans also sculpted animals out of stone, animal bones, and horns.

Stone Age people built different kinds of shelters according to the area and climate. Early humans often lived in caves, in the shelters of cliffs, or on the edges of rivers. Sometimes they made huts of stone or mammoth bones, or teepees covered with animal skins. Inside these shelters, the lives of Stone Age people centered around the fire. They cooked with it, gathered around it to tell stories, and slept next to it.

An early family

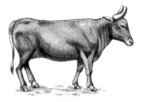

The ancestor of the cow was the aurochs, a fierce, solid, and agile animal with long horns.

The ancestor of the pig was the wild boar, while the ancestor of the sheep was the mouflon.

About 10,000 years ago the world changed. The glaciers melted. Some animals, such as the mammoth, became extinct. In the Tigris and Euphrates valleys, people began to capture wild cattle, sheep, and pigs to domesticate them.

People were also becoming farmers. They learned to plant wheat and barley seeds in the soil and harvest these crops. In North and South America, farmers raised maize, or corn. People established villages near the pastures and fields.

This new way of life allowed people to stay in one place. It gave them more time to develop other skills such as pottery and weaving. In the villages, people built granaries to store their food. All the villagers had enough food, but now they had to protect it.

An early farming village

Early agricultural tools

The birth of war

Tribes had always fought amongst themselves, but now whole armies were forming. Warriors with bronze swords came from great distances on their horses to raid the villages. These soldiers took slaves and set themselves up as leaders. When these leaders died, they were sometimes buried in large tombs with their swords and jewels.

Inside the village

Craftsmen worked with wood and metal. Other artisans made pottery and wove fabric from wool.

From agriculture to the Iron Age

The first looms were set on the ground or against a wall.

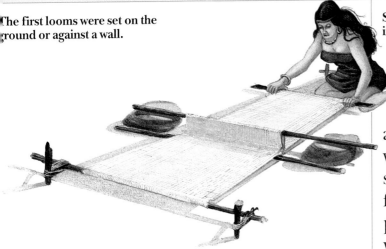

Stonehenge was built as a religious center in England about 4,000 years ago.

Iron Age

Three to four thousand years ago, people invented ovens in which to make iron. This metal slowly replaced bronze, especially for heavy tools and weapons. By 500 B.C., people throughout Europe used iron. It wasn't used in North and South America until the Europeans brought it over.

Weaving allowed people to make better clothes. By about 7000 B.C., people in the Middle East were making linen from the straw of the flax they raised. They also learned to make yarn from the wool of sheep. The Chinese had learned to make clothing from silk by 2600 B.C.

Pottery

As people perfected weaving, they were able to make finer and more beautiful fabrics. They used extracts from plants and flowers to dye the cloth.

Bronze Age

People had been making tools from copper for many years. Then someone discovered that mixing copper with tin produced a stronger metal: bronze. With this new metal, workers made fine weapons and tools. This discovery led to the development of trade with neighboring people for the raw materials needed to make bronze.

To heat up the flames in the oven where iron was made, metalworkers blew down long tubes or used bellows. The impurities ran out a hole, and the metal settled in the bottom of the oven.

Egypt during the time of the pharaohs

Egypt was one of the earliest civilizations. It dates back to about 4000 B.C. This desert nation was one of the richest in the world. The Nile River ran through Egypt, irrigating its fertile valley. Kings called pharaohs ruled Egypt. The Egyptians built magnificent temples, pyramids, and palaces to honor the pharaoh and the gods.

Life on the Nile

Egyptian life centered around the Nile. Each year, it overflowed its banks and flooded the fields of its valley. People built their houses along the river on high ground to keep them safe from the floodwaters. After the Nile receded, the fields were moist and covered with a fresh layer of fertile mud. The farmers could then plant their crops, which would grow well in this soil.

Child's toy

Egyptians used throwing sticks to hunt ducks and geese along the Nile River. People netted fish from the river to feed their families or to sell in the markets.

A rich culture developed along the banks of the Nile River.

Leisure time in Egypt

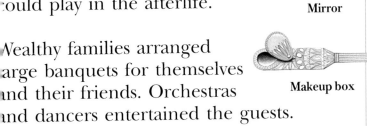

Pickax

Dice games, jacks, and checkers were some of the favorite pastimes of the ancient Egyptians. People sometimes had their game pieces buried with them when they died; they believed they could play in the afterlife.

Mirror

Wealthy families arranged large banquets for themselves and their friends. Orchestras and dancers entertained the guests. The musicians played harps, lyres, drums, and flutes. The singers shook rattles and clapped to keep time with the music.

Makeup box

How did the Egyptians dress? Men wore loincloths and women dressed in long linen robes. They either went barefoot or wore sandals made of leather or papyrus. The children often went undressed. Egyptian men and women wore wigs for ceremonies. Children's heads were shaved, except for a lock of hair on the right side of the scalp.

The homes of the Egyptians

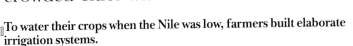

were built of brick painted in bright colors. Only wealthy families might have gardens growing around a pool and granaries for storing food. Most people lived in crowded cities with little room.

To water their crops when the Nile was low, farmers built elaborate irrigation systems.

The Egyptians believed their pharaoh was a god.

The pharaohs had many servants.

People often gave the pharaohs gifts.

They built temples and palaces.

They loved to go on hunting safaris.

Because of his strong and well-organized army, the pharaoh could keep peace in Egypt.

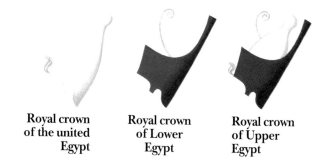

Royal crown of the united Egypt

Royal crown of Lower Egypt

Royal crown of Upper Egypt

The pharaoh was a king, but was considered a god by his people. The Egyptians believed he was the son of the most powerful of gods: Ra, the sun god. Stone statues of the pharaoh were placed in front of temples. He often wore a blue and yellow striped headdress called a *nemes* and a false beard attached to his chin. He wore an ornament in the shape of a cobra on his forehead. The double crown the pharaoh wore represented his authority over Lower and Upper Egypt.

Scribes helped the pharaoh. All over Egypt thousands of scribes oversaw the crops and the temple constructions. Sometimes they went along on expeditions into the desert to bring back precious metals. Scribes were in charge of keeping the books on fine rolls of paper called papyrus.

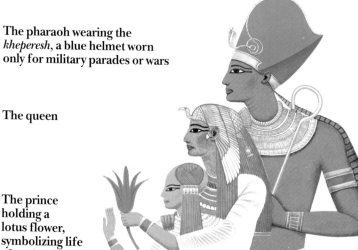

The pharaoh wearing the *kheperesh*, a blue helmet worn only for military parades or wars

The queen

The prince holding a lotus flower, symbolizing life after death

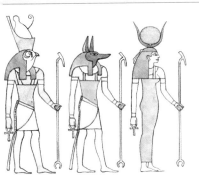

Horus   Anubis   Hathor

These characters with animals' heads and strange hairstyles were the gods who watched over Egypt. Sometimes they were represented as half-human and half-animal. Horus, the falcon-headed god, was the son of Isis and Osiris. Jackal-headed Anubis walked with the dead. Hathor, the wife of Horus and daughter of Ra, had a cow's head and was the goddess of love.

The Egyptians honored their gods with large temples. Gods had their own temple where their statue was kept. Only the priests could enter the temples. They performed rituals there three times a day, saying prayers and lighting candles to honor the gods.

The great pyramids of the pharaohs

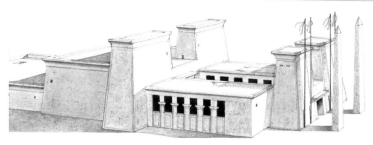

The two tall stones on each side of the entryway of the temple are called obelisks.

The pyramids of Egypt, housing the tombs of the pharaohs, stand in the desert near the Nile River. In each pyramid, secret chambers lead to a room where the sarcophagus and mummy of the pharaoh are kept. Surrounding these rooms are other rooms filled with furniture, vases, and precious objects: the treasures of the pharaoh. Pharaohs believed they could take their wealth into the next life.

The construction of a pyramid could take up to 30 years. The stone blocks used to build the pyramids sometimes came from quarries long distances away. Workers loaded the blocks onto barges and floated them down the Nile to the building site of the pyramid.

Once the barges reached the site of the pyramid, the Egyptians moved the stones across land on sleds. But the Egyptians didn't have cranes for lifting the stones into place. They probably built immense ramps all around the pyramid to allow workers to slide the stones into place.

From the desert sand, archeologists uncover the buried temples and sometimes find wonderful treasures.

The Egyptians tried to make the pyramids safe from intruders.

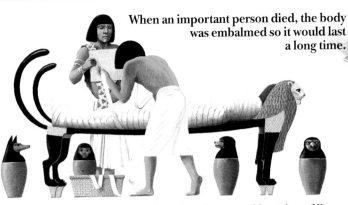

When an important person died, the body was embalmed so it would last a long time.

The body was perfumed and wrapped in strips of linen.

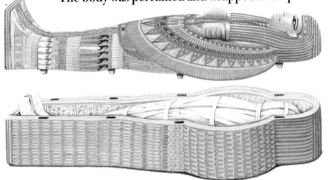

The tomb of the great king named Cheops rests in the tallest pyramid, which is 482 feet (147 m) high.

The Egyptians built the pyramids to keep thieves out.

Entryways were hidden and the galleries that led to the king's burial chamber were blocked to keep robbers from getting in. But those methods didn't always work. Robbers stole many of the treasures buried with the pharaohs.

The interiors of the pyramids resemble houses. In order for the dead to be happy there, the Egyptians believed the walls had to be decorated with paintings depicting life along the Nile. The tombs were filled with beautiful furniture and the statues of the pharaohs' favorite servants.

Roadways link the pyramids of Giza with the valley temples on the banks of the Nile.

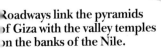

5

4

3

Cheops's pyramid
1. King's chamber
2. Queen's chamber

3. First burial chamber
4. Grand gallery
5. Air shafts

Ancient Greece's hours of glory

On the shores of the Mediterranean, there is a country where the sea is never far away—Greece. About 3,000 years ago, the Greeks established their city-states in large port towns on the coast. Their territories also included the surrounding countryside. At this time, the nation of Greece didn't exist, only the city-states which shared a common language, religion, and heritage. Athens was the most famous city-state.

The Parthenon on the Acropolis of Athens

The Persian army destroyed the temples of Athens during an invasion in 480 B.C. Thirty-two years later, the people of Athens rebuilt their temples on the Acropolis, the highest place in the city. The biggest and most beautiful temple was the Parthenon, built to honor Athena, goddess of art, wisdom, and war.

The city-states often fought wars with each other. If a different country threatened one of them, the other city-states would come to its defense.

The gods held an important place in the life of the Greeks. Before starting significant activities, the Greeks offered sacrifices to the gods to show their thankfulness. Sometimes an offering included gold or jewelry, but on certain occasions a lamb or a cow was killed on an altar. At Delphi, they built great treasuries to house the offerings made to Apollo. The Greeks also believed they could communicate with their gods through an intermediate person called an oracle.

The temple of Apollo at Delphi as it may have looked

Dionysus, god of celebration

Aphrodite, goddess of love

Greek temples were always harmonious with the landscape. Under the direction of architects, hundreds of craftsmen worked to carve and polish the marble. White columns, without any decoration, pulled the eye toward the top of the building, the pediment, and its sculpted and painted scenes. Inside, the temples were nearly empty except for the statues of the gods. Sacrifices took place outside the temple.

Many nations copied the Doric, Ionic, and Corinthian columns perfected by the Greeks.

Daily life in the city-states

Theater was popular in ancient Greece. The Greeks sometimes held competitions, often lasting from sunrise to sunset, to determine the best plays. Judges or the audience picked the winners. Theater began in Greece as a religious festival in honor of Dionysus.

Tragic plays showed how people's faults could affect their lives. The comedies playfully mocked human weaknesses.

A Greek play

A crown of leaves symbolized victory. Only the best athletes received one.

The actors wore solemn masks for tragedies and funny masks for comedies. They performed in the open air. Some of the benches the spectators sat on are still used today.

Healthy bodies were important to the Greeks. Many people worked out at the *palestra,* a public sports facility. Some men took part in boxing matches; they wore no gloves, but only leather straps to protect their fingers.

Men also participated in sports at a gymnasium, which was usually a pleasant place on the outskirts of town.

In Sparta, a rival city of Athens, girls as well as boys received athletic training. The Spartans believed this would help the girls to be better mothers to future soldiers.

Vial of oil and a strigil

After their educational training, the philosophers gathered at the gymnasium with their students. The philosophers believed that people should be healthy in body, mind, and spirit.

At the end of a workout, the athletes washed and then used the strigil to scrape the sweat, oil, and dirt from their bodies.

The Greeks took pride in being physically fit.

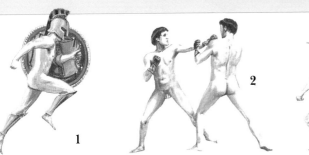
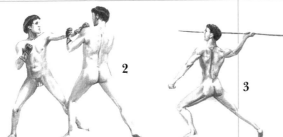

Olympic sports:
1. Races for armed warriors
2. Boxing: the hands were wrapped with leather strips.
3. Javelin throw
4. The discus throw: the thrower picked up the discus in both hands and spun around to throw it.

Many of the city-states organized games to bring together the best athletes of Greece.

People practiced the long jump while holding weights in each hand to strengthen the arm and leg muscles.

The most famous of these games was held at Olympia.

Beginning around 776 B.C., the Olympic games took place every four years and lasted five days. These ancient games serve as the model for the modern-day Olympics. The Olympics included many events, such as the popular chariot and horse racing, running, jumping, boxing, discus, javelin, and wrestling.

Children also participated in the games.

They weren't allowed to participate in violent activities such as wrestling or *pancratium,* a fierce form of fighting. They also could not enter the pentathlon, which combined jumping, the discus and javelin throw, a foot race, and wrestling.

Sports arenas were lively places in ancient Greece.

People in a Greek city-state

Greek homes were simple. The walls, made of brick or wood, had many windows. Most houses had an *andron,* a dining room used by the men to entertain their male friends. Women weren't allowed in this room while these male guests were present.

What did the women do? Young girls stayed in the home until they married. Once they married, they managed their own households. Women lived in separate quarters in the house. Here, they spent much of their time weaving and sewing. Servants often did the hardest work.

Greek vases and cooking utensils

From about the age of seven, boys went to school. They learned reading, writing, and mathematics. Girls stayed at home.

The streets of Athens were winding, narrow, and usually lively. They were often muddy because everyone threw their dirty water into them. Farmers came from the villages to sell their livestock and their fruits and vegetables in Athens. The busy streets were lined with the booths of craftsmen selling oil lamps, vases, and weapons, as well as merchants selling fruits and vegetables.

The Greek merchants left with grapes, olive oil, vases, and jewelry.

The Greeks set out on the seas to establish more city-states far from Greece and increase their wealth.

They brought back wheat from Egypt, Sicily, and the Crimean, wood from the Balkans, Ethiopian ivory, and gold and silver from Thrace.

The Greeks built communities in southern Italy, Sicily, Spain, France, and Africa. In these new lands they planted grape vines and olive trees and built towns and temples. They brought their language, money, religion, customs, science, and form of government with them.

The Greeks developed an early form of democracy, meaning that the citizens had representation in their government. To be a citizen, a person's parents had to be Greek citizens. It wasn't a true democracy because neither slaves, who made up a large part of the population, nor women could participate in government.

Prisoners taken in wars often became Greek slaves. They were bought, sold, and treated like animals. Most citizens had at least one slave to do difficult work.

As the population in Greece grew, land for cultivation became scarce. From sea-going merchants, the Greeks learned of the many rich lands beyond their shores.

In Greek democracy, each male citizen had a voice. Many other nations at this time had kings who made all the decisions.

The Romans established an empire around the Mediterranean Sea.

While the Greek city-states warred among themselves, the city of Rome grew large and spread its influence around the Mediterranean. By the time Julius Caesar became ruler of the Roman Empire, Rome had nearly one million inhabitants and ruled a large territory.

Roman citizens gathered at the forum. They came to discuss politics, trade goods, participate in religious ceremonies, or gossip. The forum was the social center of the city, and every Roman city had one.

Nearly every day, the Romans went to the public baths. But they bathed for other reasons besides cleanliness. They believed that bathing helped to purify their whole body. At these baths, the Romans also played games. Sweating was another way that Romans believed they could purify their bodies.

The Romans spent much of their time in the public arenas.

Actors performed comedies and tragedies at the theaters. Roman audiences loved the farces and mimes done with music and dance.

A Roman theater

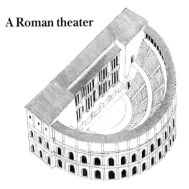

At the Coliseum in Rome and at arenas throughout the empire, performances sometimes lasted for several days. Audiences bet money on chariot races or battles between gladiators, who were often forced to fight lions, bears, and other starving wild animals. Gladiators sometimes had to fight each other to the death. They were usually slaves, prisoners of war, or criminals. But sometimes men would volunteer to fight for prize money. Even a few women fought.

City life in the Roman Empire

Roman balance

Roman cities were lively places. At night, the sound of chariots and their drivers filled the streets. During the day, people crowded the streets on their way to the markets, the baths, the forum, or the coliseum. Roman city streets were filthy. Garbage was usually dumped in the streets and left to decay. Fires and floods were common in Rome, and major earthquakes occurred an average of twice each century.

Roman education

Children learned reading, writing, law, and morality but little mathematics. Slave children learned mathematics so that they could someday become accountants or cashiers. Every child learned to speak Greek because it was the main language used throughout the empire. Teachers were usually Greek slaves.

Roman children

Roman parents wrapped their baby's elbows, knees, and ankles with a tight cloth. They believed that children must be shaped into proper adults.

Slave clothing (1, 2)
Clothes for the master and mistress (3, 4)

1   2   3   4

Roman dress

Slaves wore only a simple tunic, while male citizens wore togas over their tunics. Women wore long tunics. Men wore their togas in public when they conducted business. The color of the toga indicated the social standing of the citizen. White was for election candidates, and purple trim signified wealth.

The barber gave men haircuts, shaves, and applied cologne.

Romans loved to socialize.

Daily life in Rome

Every morning, the slaves fixed the hair and makeup of their mistress.

The Romans worshipped many gods, but Jupiter was the most powerful. Romans often held rituals in which they prayed and sacrificed cattle or goats. In this way they hoped to receive the gods' protection. Romans observed many feast days throughout the year. Each of these celebrations honored a different god. On feast days, people considered it bad luck to work.

Almost every Roman home had an altar.

In the morning, the master gave orders to the servants.

Wealthy Romans rose at dawn and worked hard until early afternoon. Slaves took care of their master's house and some of his business. In the evenings, people attended banquets and socialized at the forum. The wealthiest citizens lived the closest to the forum. The main meal of the day was dinner, called *cena*. The menu of the wealthy Roman might consist of shellfish, venison, and pastries. Poor Romans settled with vegetables and olive oil.

Romans ate dinner with the right hand while lying on a bed.

Many Roman children received their education at home.

How to drape a toga

Toga

The Roman army conquered all the lands around the Mediterranean.

Roman army life

The Roman army was made up of many legions, with about 4,000 soldiers in each. Usually Rome had no army during peace-time, only during times of war. In camp, soldiers slept in leather tents and ate mostly wheat. Meat and alcohol, they believed, would make them weak. They feasted after winning a war.

On the day of battle, the soldiers formed three lines. When the enemy advanced, the first line stepped aside and let them pass. The line then closed in behind them.

Roman ships carried wheat and other food from Egypt and luxury items from China.

Outside of the cities, farms dotted the Empire's countryside. Most farmers had slaves to care for the grapes, gather the olives for oil, or herd sheep. Every farm had oil and grape presses. Farms near cities raised asparagus, pigs, chickens, and fruit. Farmers sold much of this to people in the city. Farmers and their wives managed the farms. Single men were not allowed to own farms.

Roman politicians not only owned a house in the city but also owned one or more farms. They raised their children on the farms, away from the disease and corruption of the city.

Rome carried on trade with many countries. Much of Rome's food came from Egypt and North Africa. Romans also traded with India, China, and the barbarian tribes to the north.

Rome carried out great building projects in the lands it conquered. The Romans built roads, bridges, tunnels, and aqueducts to carry water.

The Romans imported products from all over the world.

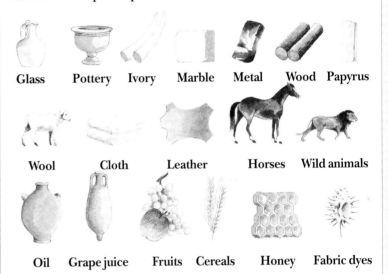

| Glass | Pottery | Ivory | Marble | Metal | Wood | Papyrus |

| Wool | Cloth | Leather | Horses | Wild animals |

| Oil | Grape juice | Fruits | Cereals | Honey | Fabric dyes |

In England, the Romans built a wall 73 miles (118 km) long to keep out invaders from the north.

The ruins of many Roman building projects still exist in Africa and Europe.

Built mainly for military use, Roman roads were durable. Some are still used today.

The barbarians invaded Rome from the north and east.

After 395 A.D., the Roman Empire was split in two: the Byzantine Empire and the Western Roman Empire. The barbarians, many different tribes of people from the East, soon invaded the borders of the Western Roman Empire. The word barbarian comes from a Greek word, *barbaros,* meaning foreign.

Beginning in 434 A.D., the armies of Attila the Hun moved eastward out of the Asiatic steppes and conquered barbarian lands in Central Europe. In order to flee these formidable warriors, the barbarians moved west into the Roman Empire.

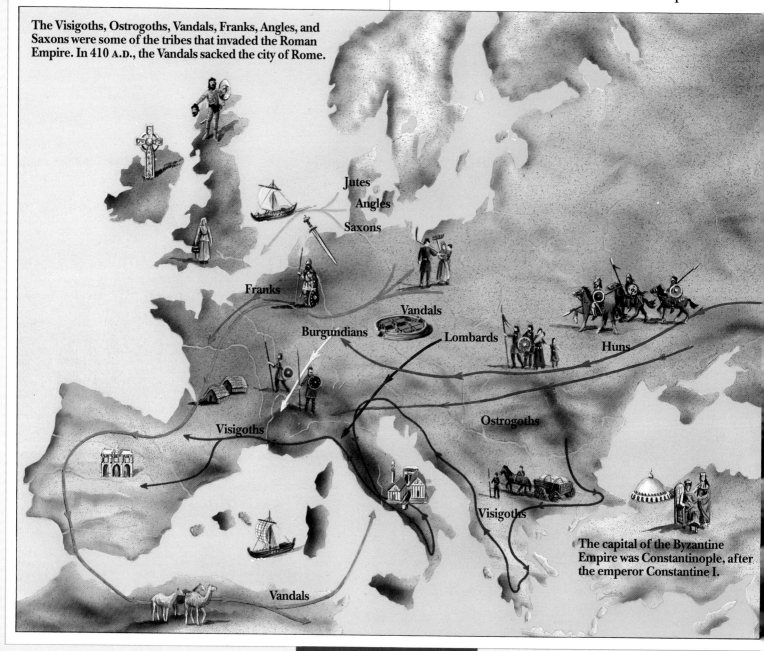

The Visigoths, Ostrogoths, Vandals, Franks, Angles, and Saxons were some of the tribes that invaded the Roman Empire. In 410 A.D., the Vandals sacked the city of Rome.

Jutes

Angles

Saxons

Franks

Vandals

Burgundians

Lombards

Huns

Ostrogoths

Visigoths

Visigoths

The capital of the Byzantine Empire was Constantinople, after the emperor Constantine I.

Vandals

The barbarians were fearless warriors. many considered it a great honor to die n battle for their cause.

Attila ruled the Huns from 434 to 453. He was a feared warrior, but a fair and just ruler for his people.

Attila the Hun forced Roman leaders to pay him tribute. In 451, the emperor Valentinian III refused to pay. Angered by this refusal, Attila attacked Gaul, but he was defeated.

In 488, an army of Ostrogoths crossed the Alps and invaded Rome.

Across Europe, Roman rule was replaced by barbarian kingdoms.

Little by little, a new society developed.
The barbarians succeeded in conquering the once-mighty Roman Empire. The barbarians and the Romans settled peacefully side by side. Europe was now many separate kingdoms. The clothing and customs of the barbarians became a mix of their own and of the Roman and Greek civilizations. Many of the barbarian people adopted the Christian religion.

The lives of barbarian men centered around fighting and hunting.

The Byzantines influenced much barbarian craft work.

Trade and craft work were important in building the old Roman civilization, but under the barbarians, agriculture became the main source of income. Skilled craftsmen now sold their goods for local use, rather than to other countries.

Barbarian punishment was sometimes brutal, such as walking on hot coals with bare feet.

In the old Roman society, several classes of people made up the citizenry, and it was possible for even the poorest Roman to be a free man. In the new barbarian world, a different class system emerged. The highest class, the aristocracy, were able to acquire land. The people under the aristocracy had to work the land, often no better off than slaves. Unlike the Romans, most of the barbarian aristocrats were violent and could neither read nor write. Petty battles between landholders were common. Sometimes entire families died in these feuds.

In the conquered countries, a new way of life emerged.

Even though trade had almost stopped, the barbarian lords loved to have the finer things in life.

Land represented the basis of all wealth.

More land also brought greater power to the lords. Barbarian lords took over old Roman properties and established new villages. They built walls around their farmland and raised wheat, goats, and sheep. The peasants were under the control of the lords.

While the peasants worked in the fields, made tools, and built houses, the lords hunted in the forests for wild boar, deer, and aurochs. The kings had little power over the lords. War was common between the lords and kings and between separate kingdoms throughout the land.

The church served as a refuge for all people. Even bandits were granted asylum there.

Like the Romans, the barbarian kings minted their own money.

Clovis, the first Christian king of the Franks, built a solid kingdom.
With the help of the priests, he converted his people to Christianity. According to Frankish law, when a king died, his heirs divided up his kingdom. When Clovis died, his four sons inherited his kingdom and lost much of the power.

Muslim invaders brought knowledge to Europe.

Three centuries after the first invasions, it was no longer possible to tell a barbarian descendant from that of a Roman citizen.

The next group to invade Europe was the Muslims. These people followed the Islamic faith, a new religion founded by the prophet Muhammad in the country known today as Saudi Arabia.

Arabic reads from right to left.

After the death of Muhammad, the Muslims went out to conquer other countries in the name of their one god, who they called Allah. They already ruled a vast empire from India to Africa by the time they set their sights on Europe. Between 711 and 713, they fought the Visigoths and gained control of much of Spain. The Christians united under Charles Martel, the leader of the Franks. In 732, he stopped the advance of the Muslims near Poitiers in France. Martel's grandson, Charlemagne, later came to power.

Window in Arabesque style (Muslim)

The Muslims brought more than just war to Europe. They also brought their medicine, mathematics, and astronomy. Arabic numerals, still used today, replaced the Roman numerals used by Europeans at this time. The Muslims stayed in Spain for more than 700 years. Much of Spanish architecture shows the influence of the Muslims' refined culture.

The Vikings invaded Europe from the north.

Charlemagne, a Frankish king, conquered a large part of Europe. In 800, he was crowned emperor of the Western Empire. His capital at Aix-la-Chappelle, in modern Germany, became the leading cultural center in Europe.

Charlemagne wanted his noblemen to be well-educated so they would be better government servants. He recruited educated monks from Europe to establish a school at the palace.

After Charlemagne's death, his empire was split among his ancestors. This weakened Europe against its enemies. The Vikings took advantage of this weakness and for 300 years attacked the towns and monasteries of England and Europe. To keep the Vikings from destroying all of France, the French king gave them land on the coast. This land became known as the land of the Northmen, or Normandy.

Charlemagne

The Vikings came from the north to attack Europe. They first raided England and Ireland. All over Europe people prayed, "From the fury of the Northmen, deliver me, Lord," but the Vikings weren't all bad. They built trading posts and colonized Greenland.

Lords built castles to defend their land.

Castles remind us of a time full of danger, when highwaymen and warriors pillaged towns and the countryside. Often the lords of these castles fought among themselves. The kings usually weren't powerful enough to keep the peace.

The first castles were simple wooden structures with only a tower and walls. Fire often destroyed them. Then in the 12th century, the lords began to build their castles with stone. Some of the walls of these stone castles were 25 feet (8 m) thick and 125 feet (38 m) high.

Parts of early wooden castles or fortresses

The construction of castles could take many years to complete. As the centuries passed and building techniques improved, castles became bigger and stronger.

In the Middle Ages, powerful lords controlled large areas of land and ruled over the countryside. They used castles to protect their lands, and many lords had more than one castle. Castles were defended by archers who shot arrows or by guards who dumped hot oil from the walls onto the enemy below. The development of gunpowder and powerful cannons made castles unnecessary, but many of the architectural techiques of this time are still in use.

The ruins of these old castles still dot the countryside throughout most of Europe.

1. Moat
2. Rampart
3. Parapet
4. Crenelation
5. Parapet walk
6. Loophole
7. Barbican
8. Drawbridge
9. Fortification wall
10. Machicolation
11. Keep

Life inside the castle

The lord of the castle sometimes hosted feasts. He often served venison, pork, mutton, salmon, and sardines. Meat in the Middle Ages spoiled quickly; it was heavily spiced to hide the bad taste.

The peasants didn't eat meat. In England, the peasants ate beans, bread, and cheese. In Germany they ate sauerkraut and porridge. Raw fruits, believed unwholesome, weren't eaten by people in the Middle Ages.

To amuse the lord's guests, jugglers and acrobats put on shows, and troubadours recited poems. Minstrels sang while playing lutes, harps, or tambourines. The guests sang and danced. Meanwhile, crowds of servants kept busy preparing the feast in the kitchen. The chief cook supervised the meal's creation.

Eating utensils of the Middle Ages

Much of the nobleman's life centered around hunting and fighting.

Knights were professional soldiers who started their careers early. The men first had to spend years as shield bearers for their lords, learning the art of war. They became knights once they had learned to fight and could afford the equipment.

The lords loved hunting with falcons. The bird would fly up and spot a rabbit, which it would dive down upon and kill. The falcon then would come back to sit on the gloved hand of its master. The lords hunted for amusement and to have wild game to eat. Peasants could hunt only small animals.

At tournaments, knights would show off their horsemanship and their skill with weapons. These tournaments were training for war, but they became social events as well. Fortune-tellers, harness makers, horse dealers, and moneylenders sold their products to the crowds.

Peasants had a hard life in the Middle Ages.

Peasants, called serfs, were bound in duty to their lord. They worked the lord's land, and in exchange, the lord gave them lodging and fields of their own to cultivate. He protected them and sheltered them in his castle in times of danger, and in return, they were expected to help defend it.

The castle, peasants' dwellings, and surrounding fields made up the lord's manor.

The lord cut down the trees of his forest to make room for wheat fields.

Life in the Middle Ages centered around the manor, which consisted of the castle and everything around it owned by the lord. This included the land, the peasants' homes, the villages, and the common ground where everyone could graze their livestock and gather wood.

The life of the peasants was hard. They had to pay rent—usually a pig or a couple of chickens, and sometimes half their crops—to the lord for their small houses. They also were required to give 10 percent of their small crop to the parish priest to pay his wages and to pay for upkeep of the church.

Disease made life hard for everyone. In 1347, the bubonic plague, or Black Death, spread across Europe. Between 1347 and 1350, as much as one-third of Europe's population died from this disease.

Rats spread the Black Death throughout Europe as they moved from one town to the next.

The roles of the lord and monks

The lord made the law of the manor. He could send anyone who disobeyed his law to jail. He protected and watched over the serfs who depended on him for their homes and land, but he also forced them to defend his property against enemies.

Grape press

Bread oven

The lady of the castle supervised the house and managed the manor in her husband's absence. She ordered provisions, supervised meal preparation, and oversaw the servants. She made sure her children did their schoolwork.

Many women's fathers had to pay a dowry in the form of money or land to the family of the men their daughters married. Some families considered their daughters a burden. If a daughter couldn't find a husband, her family might send her to a convent to live. Then they would not have to support her.

Before the invention of the printing press, monks in the monasteries copied and illustrated books by hand.

The monasteries had an important role during the Middle Ages. Monasteries were often rich and owned much land. After the age of five, many boys of the noble class lived in the monasteries. There they spent their lives praying, studying the Bible, and doing good works. They learned to speak and write in Latin. Many monasteries also ran schools for the children of wealthier families. In most European countries, these were the only schools available at the time.

Craftsmen and merchants began to form guilds.

During the 12th and 13th centuries, towns and cities began to develop. Villages had always existed, but with the growing power of the merchant and craftsman classes, villages became larger. The craftsmen made many things, such as jewelry, shoes, or tools. The merchants grew rich importing silk, spices, and other goods. The craftsmen and merchants formed groups called guilds, which helped their members and regulated the way they did business. As the guilds became more powerful, they bought charters from the lords to give them their freedom from the manor.

The market square of a town was a busy place. Much of the business and social activity of a town happened there. People came to buy and sell their goods, pay their taxes, socialize, and worship. The town hall, church, and bell tower surrounded the market square.

People in Middle Age towns threw their garbage into the narrow streets. Houses were built close together and made of wood. In their dark and gloomy homes, people slept on straw mattresses. Fires often destroyed large parts of the towns.

Peasants still worked the fields outside the city walls.

Some villages grew into cities.

Until the 12th century, most education took place in the monasteries. With the knowledge of the ancient Greek world brought to Europe by the Muslims, there became a demand for more schools. The increase in trade and larger governments required more educated people. Cathedrals and towns began to build schools to prepare the children for life in this more complicated world. Students studied Latin because most writing was still done in this language.

By the 13th century, cities began to build universities. At first, universities held classes in rented halls, and students had to rent rooms in private homes. The first university to own its own buildings and provide housing for students was the University of Paris. It soon became a model for other developing universities.

The cities began to grow. With the increase in trade, more jobs were created, and people began to leave the countryside for the city. By 1300, Paris had a population of 80,000 while London had a population of 50,000. Many of these people lived in houses made of wood. On the main floor of some homes, a shop or a workshop opened onto the street. The narrow streets were rarely paved. When it rained, they became muddy, making it hard for people and horses to get around. At night, unlit roads became dangerous because of the criminals who wandered them.

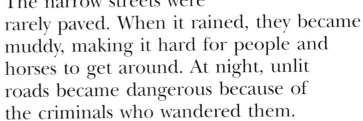

Beginning in the 14th and 15th centuries, Western civilization began to develop more quickly. This period is known as the Renaissance, a French word meaning "rebirth." People of the Renaissance made great progress in literature, science, and art. Traveling by sea, Europeans discovered faraway lands.

In the 1450s, Johannes Gutenburg printed a Bible using a printing press with movable type, the first use of this invention in Europe. Hundreds of copies of books could now be printed in the time it took the monks to copy one by hand, making books cheaper and more available.

Powerful weapons were developed.

The long voyages

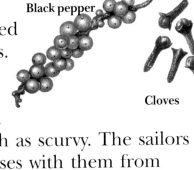

Astrolabe

European nations of the 15th century traded with many other countries. Spices and silk brought from India and other countries in the East sold for high prices. European nations began to send ships out on the oceans to search for gold and other precious metals in far-off lands. Looking for a western route that would lead to India, Christopher Columbus landed in the Bahamas in 1492. Europeans soon established colonies to exploit the riches of this new world. They conquered the native people and forced many of them to give up their old customs. At the same time, the Portuguese, the British, and the Dutch left for India to establish colonies there.

These dangerous voyages often lasted two or three years. Because of their poor diet, many sailors died at sea from diseases such as scurvy. The sailors also carried illnesses with them from Europe to the new lands. The native people had no resistance to these diseases, so many of them died.

Black pepper

Cloves

Art and education flourished during the Renaissance.

Statue of a discus thrower

The Italian cities grew rich from these trips to the Orient. The powerful families who governed these cities sometimes lent money to kings and the pope. These wealthy families established banks in cities across Europe. Merchants borrowed money from these banks as they traveled. They no longer had to carry money and worry about thieves trying to rob them.

The Renaissance brought about a renewed interest in Greek and Roman art. Artists imitated the sculpture and architecture of these early civilizations. Many people began to collect artwork of that time and search for Greek and Latin manuscripts that had been forgotten in monasteries for centuries.

More people became educated. The business of governments was still conducted in Latin, but more and more, authors wrote books in the language of the people. Being literate in their own languages allowed more people to exchange ideas.

The Renaissance leaders were refined and elegant, but often cruel. In the Italian city of Florence, Lorenzo de Medici ran a banking house and ruled the city. He lived surrounded by musicians, painters, writers, and scholars. He hired Europe's greatest architects and artists to build his mansions and create beautiful works of art. In 1478, rivals of Lorenzo de Medici tried to remove him from power by murdering him. They failed, and de Medici sought revenge by brutally killing many of the people he believed had planned his murder.

Great progress was made in the arts and sciences during the Renaissance.

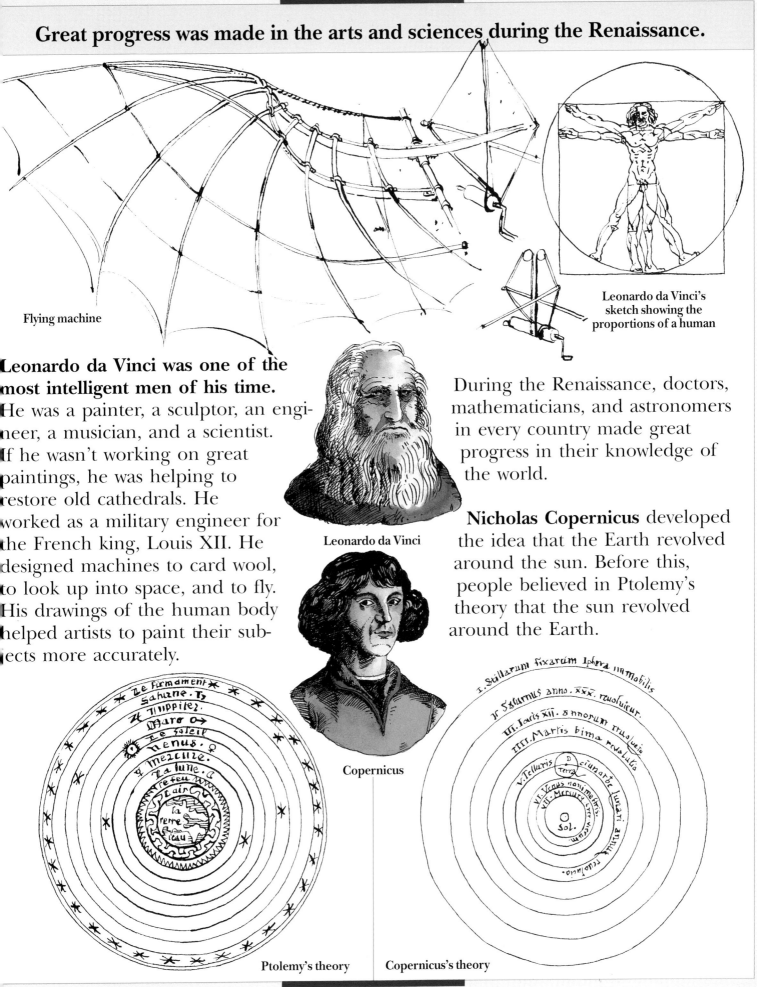

Flying machine

Leonardo da Vinci's sketch showing the proportions of a human

Leonardo da Vinci was one of the most intelligent men of his time. He was a painter, a sculptor, an engineer, a musician, and a scientist. If he wasn't working on great paintings, he was helping to restore old cathedrals. He worked as a military engineer for the French king, Louis XII. He designed machines to card wool, to look up into space, and to fly. His drawings of the human body helped artists to paint their subjects more accurately.

Leonardo da Vinci

During the Renaissance, doctors, mathematicians, and astronomers in every country made great progress in their knowledge of the world.

Nicholas Copernicus developed the idea that the Earth revolved around the sun. Before this, people believed in Ptolemy's theory that the sun revolved around the Earth.

Copernicus

Ptolemy's theory

Copernicus's theory

43

During the 17th and 18th centuries, European kings became more powerful.

Since the Middle Ages, kings had ruled most of the nations of Europe. In many countries, a son succeeded his father as heir to the nation's throne.

A king lived in a palace with his family: the queen, their children, his brothers, their uncles, and their cousins. They, and the crowds of advisors, servants, friends, and guests, made up the court.

In the 17th century, Louis XIV's court numbered in the thousands and stretched for miles as it traveled with many possessions from one palace to another.

Depending on the season, the king would stay in a different palace, and when he traveled, he brought his court along. Wagons carried the furniture, and mules carried trunks filled with clothes and dishes. During this time, European royalty tried to show its power by building splendid palaces.

An army of servants took care of the needs of the court.

Under Louis XIV's rule, France became the most powerful nation in Europe. Louis loved to show off his great power by hiring the best artists and architects to build and decorate his palaces. His greatest project, the Palace of Versailles, was begun in 1669. Versailles was originally a royal hunting lodge located 11 miles (18 km) outside of Paris. Eventually, it became the seat of government in France and the royal residence for more than 100 years.

Building wasn't the only way Louis tried to display his power. He often warred with other European countries. By the end of his reign, Louis had to melt down silver from his palace and sell it to pay for these expensive wars.

Fashion accessories of the French court

The most talented artists designed the gardens and decorated the facades. Columns and statues decorated the buildings and courtyards of the palace. Sculpted terraces circled the roofs of buildings. King Louis XIV loved to hold lavish parties and banquets in the beautiful palace gardens.

Many European kings tried to copy the splendor of Versailles.

Life was still hard for the lower classes in the 17th and 18th centuries.

At the age of eight, Mozart was invited to Versailles to play the harpsichord for the king.

In all the royal courts of Europe, ballets, operas, and plays were an important part of life. The royal families paid the artists and musicians to paint the family portraits or to perform at the palaces. Without the money of the wealthy class, much of the world's art would not exist.

But working-class people still led a hard life. They worked hard just to have something to eat. When the wheat crops failed in the countryside, the price of bread went up in the towns. By the 1600s, food in some countries cost six times what it did 100 years before, while wages stayed almost the same. This made life even harder for poor people. If people couldn't pay their debts, they could be thrown in prison.

People still used water directly from rivers, where they also dumped their waste. This polluted water helped spread disease.

Captain James Cook, a British navigator, discovered Australia and Hawaii in the 18th century.

People made great progress in science and philosophy. Many philosophers began to write about the unfair privileges of the royalty, and sometimes the officers of the king burned the philosophers' books. Still, in the meeting rooms of Europe, people continued discussing the philosophers' ideas about science, progress, and liberty.

At this time, a philosopher named Denis Diderot, along with almost 200 other philosophers and scholars, began work on an encyclopedia. This word comes from the Greek and means "general education." The philosophers wanted to compile, in alphabetical order, everything that 18th century people knew. Its first volume was published in 1751, but the entire encyclopedia wasn't completed until 1772.

In the encyclopedia's 28 volumes, people could read articles on thousands of topics from gold mining and dressmaking to art and medicine. Diderot wanted the encyclopedia not only to educate people, but also to show them that they could improve their lives by using reason.

Little by little, people began to have a better understanding of the world. Geographers drew maps of the world as it really looked, not as they imagined it. European nations established colonies around the world and introduced their discoveries to the Old World. The colonies exported tea, chocolate, potatoes, tomatoes, corn, and tobacco to their home countries. Merchants grew rich from this trade and built homes that compared with those of the aristocrats.

French botanist Antoine Parmentier persuaded Louis XVI to encourage the cultivation of potatoes since its value as a food was unknown before this time.

But not all people prospered from this new wealth. Large ships left Africa for Europe and the colonies of the New World. They sailed with a cargo of people to sell as slaves to the cotton and sugar cane plantations. These slaves suffered horrible conditions and many died on the ships. Those that reached the shore faced being separated from their families.

Some nations began to revolt against the privileged classes.

In America and France, people had become weary of the old forms of government where kings and wealthy aristocrats made all the decisions. On July 4, 1776, the 13 American colonies declared their independence from Britain after years of war. In July 1789, the French Revolution began.

The United States' *Declaration of Independence* inspired the French to write *The Declaration of the Rights of Man and Citizen.*

Both documents proclaimed that all citizens have equality in the eyes of the law and the right to live in freedom.

The French people armed themselves and attacked the castles and royal prisons. They executed King Louis XVI.

On July 14, 1789, French citizens attacked the Bastille, a prison in Paris that was a symbol of the power of the king. The French people celebrate Bastille Day each year.

Scientific achievements changed the world.

The first bicycle, called the "wooden horse," was invented in 1790 in Paris. The rider sat on it and pushed it with his feet.

Scientific discoveries and inventions happened at a faster rate than ever before.

The invention of the telegraph and Morse code permitted messages to be sent quickly. Steam engines powered trains and factories. Hot air balloons allowed people to fly for the first time. In 1784, Henry Cavendish, a British physicist, proved that water was made up of hydrogen and oxygen. A smallpox vaccination was also developed around this time.

The birth of the metric system

Until the 18th century, units of measurement around the world varied from region to region and often caused problems. In 1799, France's National Convention accepted the basic units of measurement as the meter and the gram. Most countries, except Britain and the United States, soon adopted the new metric system.

The metric system allows people to convert from one unit of measurement to the next in multiples of 10. For example, 10 millimeters equals one centimeter, 10 centimeters equals one decimeter, and 10 decimeters equals one meter.

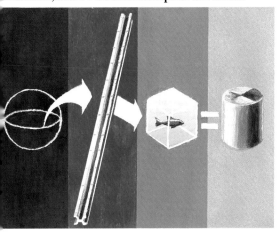

The imaginary lines passing through the North and South Poles are called meridians.

In 1793, Eli Whitney invented the cotton gin. This machine made the separation of cotton fiber from the seed much easier—and cheaper. It also made cotton production more profitable. Whitney also built the first factory to produce muskets with interchangeable parts.

Thanks to advances in surveying, more accurate maps could also be made.

49

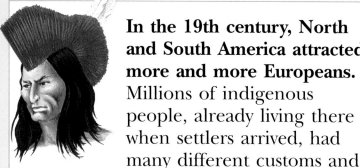

In the 19th century, North and South America attracted more and more Europeans. Millions of indigenous people, already living there when settlers arrived, had many different customs and languages. As the demand for land grew, white settlers in the United States forced the Native Americans from their land.

In the villages of the Dakota, women prepared the food, made the clothing, and set up the teepees. The men hunted buffalo and other game and defended the village. The Dakota considered the Black Hills of South Dakota sacred, but were forced to leave the area after gold was discovered there in 1874.

During the last ice age, ancestors of the Native Americans came from Asia looking for more abundant game.

The Europeans began to settle the plains.

The Mayflower

Europeans trading with the Native Americans

Herds of buffalo numbering in the millions lived on the plains of North America. These wild and powerful animals weighed more than one ton (.9 t).

The Native Americans of the plains used every part of the buffalo. They ate its meat. From its hides they made their teepees and blankets, and from its bones they made tools.

The first Europeans who arrived were fur traders. In exchange for furs, these traders would give the Native Americans metal tools and knives, wool blankets, and guns. The traders also accidentally brought diseases with them. In 1837, 15,000 people of the Mandan, Arikara, and Hidatsa tribes died in a smallpox epidemic.

As more and more settlers arrived, the Native Americans began to fight back. They attacked wagon trains and tried to keep the settlers off of their land.

When this happened, the army was sent to protect the settlers and persuade Native Americans to give up their traditional homelands. Many Native Americans died before they signed treaties to give up their land and live on reservations.

Europeans sought new opportunities in the American West.

In 1842, 120 settlers in covered wagons made the trip between Missouri and the Oregon Territory. By the 1870s, thousands of families would make the trip in search of land and opportunity.

Many wagon trains hired experienced frontiersmen to guide them. Neither this, nor the advice they received before they left, prepared them for the hardships ahead. There were rivers to cross and mountains to climb. Diseases sometimes struck the wagon train and killed many of the settlers.  At first the Native Americans encountered along the trail posed little danger to the well-armed settlers. When they did appear, it was usually to trade their buffalo meat for the settlers' tobacco, coffee, or sugar. After a six-month trip in wagons pulled by oxen or horses, the settlers arrived in Oregon. But the work was far from over.

A new home

The settlers built their farms and towns in the fertile river valleys of Oregon, home-steading this free land. The homesteaders had to be good at everything to survive: farming, hunting, and woodworking. They had to know how to cut down a tree, how to build a cabin, and how to fix a plow. Few of the first settlers got rich from their new land, and many endured rough times.

Not all those who left the East, however, made it to Oregon. Thousands took advantage of the Homestead Act of 1862 and settled in Kansas and Nebraska.

In 1845, settlers founded the city of Portland, Oregon. Two New Englanders flipped a coin, and the winner named the town after the eastern city of Portland, Maine.

Pioneers settle the West.

In 1848, a man helping to build a sawmill along a creek in California saw something yellow sparkling in the water. Gold! The cry went out around the world, and by the end of 1849, as many as 50,000 people had made the trip to California in search of instant wealth. Many Oregonians gave up their hard-won homesteads and traveled south.

As the West became settled, people elected sheriffs to establish laws and keep order in the town.

These fortune-seekers became known as the forty-niners. Few became wealthy.

Overnight, towns sprang up near the mining camps. When the mines came up empty, the people packed up and left, leaving ghost towns.

Cattle drives

The southern Great Plains were perfect for raising cattle. Each year ranchers herded thousands of cattle to railways to be shipped to eastern cities.

Miners panning for gold in California

In 1869, the first transcontinental railroad was completed across the United States. The trip to the West that once took months became much quicker. Soon other railroads built lines to the West, making settlement easier and less hazardous than in the past.

The Industrial Revolution

The Industrial Revolution started in England around 1750 and soon spread to Europe and North America. New inventions such as the steam engine turned societies away from agriculture as their main source of income. Items once made at home could now be mass-produced more cheaply in factories.

Tractors allowed farmers to cultivate more land with less help.

With railroads fast becoming the main form of transportation, large supplies of steel became necessary to make the tracks. New steel mills met this demand. Thousands of farmers left the land and moved to the cities to work in these mills.

During the Industrial Revolution, people began to find many uses for the steam engine, such as running factories and powering ships, locomotives, and farm equipment. Steam engines produced their power by burning coal. The number of jobs increased in coal mines and in the factories that built the steam engines.

In 1819, a steamboat called the Savannah became the first steam-powered ship to cross the Atlantic Ocean.

The Industrial Revolution changed the way many people lived.

Workers' housing in the 19th century

Steam locomotives carried raw materials to the factories and finished products from the factories to the market.

Factories soon began to make everything from trains to clothes. People moved to the cities for factory work, but their new city lives often became more difficult than their old farm lives. People worked long hours around dangerous equipment for little pay. If they got hurt, the factory owners did not take care of them. Many children were forced to work to help the family to survive.

The workers in the factory towns lived in small houses or apartments. The factories in these towns burned large amounts of coal and polluted the air. Eventually, the forming of trade unions and the passing of laws helped to improve the working conditions and wages of factory workers.

People who made their living at home could no longer compete with the factories.

In 1801, Joseph Jacquard invented an automatic loom that simplified the job of weaving.

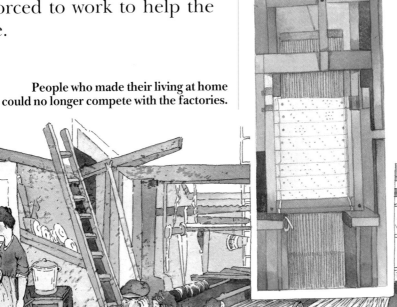

Progress after the Industrial Revolution

Technology has allowed machines, instead of people, to do some dangerous jobs in factories.

By the end of the 19th century, new technologies had improved the standard of living for most people in the industrialized nations.

Steel, a strong metal alloy made of iron and carbon, was used more than ever to build railroads, bridges, and skyscrapers.

In 1876, Alexander Graham Bell's invention of the telephone made long-distance communication much easier and quicker.

In 1879, Thomas Edison invented the light bulb. Electricity soon lit streets, houses, and factories and began to replace the steam engine as a way to power some factories' machines. In 1881, New York City installed the first power plant to supply electricity city-wide. By the end of the century, telephones and electric lights were common sights in the cities.

Doctors came to the schools to examine children.

Greater comfort in town living
By the beginning of the 20th century, life was much more comfortable than it had been a century before.

The health of people had improved.
Medical discoveries made it possible to live longer, healthier lives. Louis Pasteur, a French chemist, developed vaccines for rabies and anthrax. He also developed pasteurization. This process heats food to kill microorganisms that could be harmful to humans. In 1865, Joseph Lister first used an antiseptic to stop the infection of open wounds after surgery. This discovery made operating much safer.

More people became educated.
With rising wages in the factories and the passing of child labor laws, children no longer had to work to help support the family. Industrialized nations, such as the United States, Canada, and Great Britain, began to provide public education for their children.

Electric lamps replaced gas lamps.

New inventions made life easier.
People could now use refrigerators to keep their food from spoiling. Before this, people kept food on ice in an icebox. Air conditioners cooled the offices of the new skyscrapers. Automobiles made travel more convenient. The radio provided endless hours of entertainment.

The need for electricity to power many of the new inventions increased, and large dams were built to harness the energy of rivers. A system was set-up in 1935 to help bring electricity to rural areas in the U.S.

New inventions continue to improve the quality of our lives.

Because of radar, ships no longer have to rely only on lighthouses for their safety.

People continue to invent new ways to improve our lives. New inventions replace old ones, such as televisions, computers, CD players, cellular phones—the list seems endless. One CD-ROM can hold as much information as 28 volumes of a printed encyclopedia. Fax machines can send and receive documents in moments, a process that used to take days by mail. Satellites can send information around the world in seconds or take pictures of Earth and send them back for scientists to study. Scientists also research other planets with this technology.

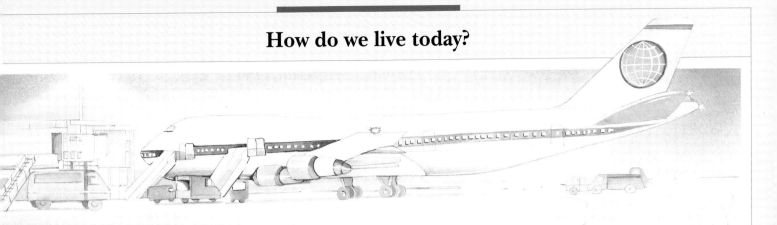

Researchers continue to make great strides in medicine. Illnesses that once claimed thousands of lives are now treated with a single visit to the doctor.

Distance is no longer the problem it once was. The Concorde supersonic jet can carry passengers at twice the speed of sound. In 1957, the Soviet Union put the first artificial satellite into orbit around Earth. In 1969, Neil Armstrong became the first person to walk on the moon. Now the development of space stations and orbiting telescopes allows us to study other planets and galaxies.

But progress comes with problems. Nuclear energy can produce electricity or make powerful bombs. The cars we drive make travel easier, but they also cause air pollution that may change our climate.

What does the future hold?

Jets can take us around the world in hours.

Travel from one country to the next has never been so easy.

News travels quickly all over the world.

Intriguing facts, activities, games, a quiz, a glossary, and addresses of places to visit, followed by the index

■ Time line

Stone Age people paint the walls of Lascaux.

Humans develop agriculture and domesticate livestock.

The Egyptians build the pyramids.

The Athenians build the Parthenon.

Rome establishes its empire.

The barbarians invade Roman territory.

Charlemagne leads the Western Empire.

Europeans build the first stone castles.

Bishops have cathedrals and abbeys constructed.

Europe discovers the New World.

Louis XIV builds Versailles.

The Enlightenment

The Industrial Revolution

15000 B.C.

Humans are nomadic hunters and gatherers.

Prehistory

10000 B.C.

4000 B.C.

Humans invent written language.

2500 B.C.   **Greco-Roman Period**

450 B.C.

1 A.D.   **Birth of Christ**

500 A.D.

800 A.D.

1000 A.D.   **Middle Ages**

1400 A.D.   Gutenberg invents movable type.

Renaissance

1600 A.D.
1700 A.D.
1800 A.D.

The modern world

1900 A.D.

■ Did you know?

We count the years from the birth of Christ.

In 525, a Roman theologian named Dionysius Exiguus incorrectly calculated Christ's birthday as December 25, 753 years after the founding of Rome. The error has remained on our calendar ever since. We also now know that Christ was actually born between 8 B.C. and 4 B.C., not the year 1 A.D.

A decade equals 10 years.
A score equals 20 years.
A century equals 100 years.
A millennium equals 1,000 years.

Learn how to count the centuries

Christopher Columbus landed in the Bahamas in 1492. Do you know why that date is in the 15th century?

The first century began with the year 1 and ended at the year 99. The second century started at the year 100 and went to 199, and so it continues.

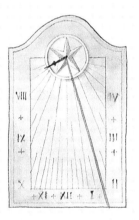

Where does the word "calendar" come from?

The *calends* for the Romans were the first days of any month. The calend of January was the same as New Year's Day. The Romans would celebrate the new year with sacrifices, presents, and good wishes.

Can you solve this problem?

There is an old chair that is one century, one score, and three decades old. How old is the chair?

Answer: It is 150 years old.

■ Food from long ago

Would our ancestors like to eat french fries and hamburgers and drink soda pop?

Would you like to eat the spicy, spoiling meats of a Middle Age feast, the cabbage and turnip stew, or the drinks sweetened with honey? People in the Middle Ages sometimes cooked swans with the feathers on.

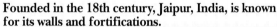
Founded in the 18th century, Jaipur, India, is known for its walls and fortifications.

Before refrigerators, people used other methods of food preservation.

Pork and herring were salted. Other fish and meats were smoked. People could store dried fruits and vegetables all winter long.

The peasants enjoyed few feasts. They ate bread, cheese, and soups. During slaughtering season, they had ham and bacon. Fish was one of their main sources of protein. In England, people ate sheep stomachs stuffed with eggs, vegetables, bread, cheese, and pork.

Tomatoes, potatoes, corn, pumpkins, and many other foods were introduced in Europe after the trips to the New World during the Renaissance. Potatoes and tomatoes were first used in Europe as ornamental plants.

■ Did you know?

Throughout history, men and women have enjoyed dressing up.

Prehistoric people made jewelry and decorated their clothes with pearls and seashells.

The Greeks and Romans fastened their clothing with ornamented clasps called *fibulas*. In public, male Roman citizens wore togas. The type of toga a Roman man wore revealed his status.

Native Americans made their moccasins of deer skin and often decorated them with porcupine quills or glass beads.

In the early part of the Middle Ages, the nobility and the peasants wore similar clothing. The nobility set themselves apart from the peasants by wearing a lot of jewelry. Later, as finer fabrics became available, police patrolled for peasants wearing elite fashions.

Men in the Middle Ages wore long cloaks fastened with a brooch or cord.

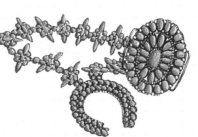

During the Renaissance, most women wanted to have golden hair. Many of them dyed or bleached their hair or wore wigs.

Men of the Renaissance almost always wore hats. They usually went clean-shaven until Henry VIII of England made beards and mustaches fashionable in the early 1500s.

Work clothes
In 1874, Levi Strauss began producing blue jeans held together with copper rivets.

From head to toe

In ancient Greece, all women had long hair, except for slaves. They usually wore it tied up in a bun. Often, men and women wore similar clothing made from rectangles of wool or linen and fastened with fibulas. Greeks typically did not display their wealth with jewelry.

In the Middle Ages, men and women wore stockings made of either wool or silk, depending on how rich they were.

Women of the Middle Ages wore makeup that had a lead base. The lead seeped into their skin and caused painful disorders and sometimes madness.

Egyptian men and women both wore eye makeup. They spent much of their time on personal grooming. Egyptians used lotions to make their hair soft and shiny and wore perfumes and jewelry. The wealthiest Egyptians had stylists fix their hair. They also had their own shops and artisans to make clothing, jewelry, and other items.

The history of perfume.
Perfumes were first developed by the ancient Egyptians, Chinese, and Palestinians. Their use was widespread in ancient Greece and Rome. The Crusaders took the knowledge of perfume-making back to Europe during the Middle Ages.

    The ladies in the court of Louis XIV spent a lot of time dressing themselves but rarely took a bath. The people of this time believed that water was polluted and would make them sick. Everyone wore a lot of perfume.

Renaissance men in England usually wore flat-heeled shoes made of leather, silk, or velvet. Gold or copper buckles or silk rosettes decorated their shoes.

During the Renaissance, both boys and girls dressed alike until they were five years old. They wore gowns that hung down to their feet.

Deadly windows
The walls of European castles had only a few narrow openings. These windows were just wide enough so archers could shoot arrows out of them at their enemies.

In the Middle Ages, children could play ball in the house without worrying about breaking the windows. Oiled paper or shutters, not glass, covered windows. The lack of windows made the inside of houses dark.

At the end of the Middle Ages, the first glass windows appeared in Europe, although the Romans had used glass framed in bronze to cover some of their windows hundreds of years before.

6. What did the Europeans want to buy in the Orient?
a. potatoes
b. spices and silk
c. cannons

7. Who were the Huns?
a. shepherds
b. a prehistoric tribe
c. barbarian warriors

3. Who constructed the first roads?
a. the Romans
b. the Egyptians
c. the Franks

4. What is celebrated in France on the 14th of July?
a. the end of a long war
b. the crowning of Louis XIV
c. the taking of the Bastille

5. What is papyrus?
a. lambskin
b. an instrument for studying the skies
c. a very strong paper

8. On cave walls, prehistoric people painted
a. the animals they hunted.
b. the birth of their village
c. the faces of their children.

9. The Parthenon is in
a. Rome.
b. Athens.
c. Paris.

10. Which French king built the Palace of Versailles?
a. Francois I
b. Louis XIV
c. Charles V

■ **Quiz**
Can you answer these questions? The answers are at the bottom of the next page.

1. Who built the pyramids?
a. the Egyptians
b. the Greeks
c. the Romans

2. What did Gutenberg invent?
a. the cannon
b. the printing press
c. the telegraph

11. What Renaissance man discovered that the Earth traveled around the sun?
a. Copernicus
b. Louis Pasteur
c. Charlemagne

■ True or false?
The answers are at the bottom of the page.

1. Electricity lit the Palace at Versailles.

2. Charlemagne and Julius Caesar met many times during their lives.

3. The Egyptians worshipped many different gods.

4. During the Middle Ages, people sometimes ate spoiled meat.

5. It was colder during prehistoric times than during the 20th century.

6. Thomas Edison invented the telephone.

7. Stone Age people were hunters and gatherers.

■ Can you answer these questions?

Why are the Native Americans called Indians?
Because Christopher Columbus thought he had found India when he landed in the Bahamas, he called the natives "Indians."

Columbus made four voyages to the New World, all the time thinking he was near Asia. He died in 1506, never realizing his mistake.

How is steel made?
First, iron is melted with coke, a kind of coal, at a high temperature. These two mixed together make a brittle metal. This metal is then refined by heating it again to eliminate the impurities. The finished product is called steel. Steel is often mixed with other elements to form alloys. Stainless steel, used for kitchen utensils, is a common alloy.

■ Games from times past

Children living during prehistoric times

probably played games such as house and hunting with toys made out of wood and leather. These materials don't last long, so archeologists haven't found any remains.

Egyptian children played

with wooden toys such as tops, balls, and carved animals. Archeologists have found these toys in Egyptian tombs.

Children throughout the ages

have loved to play ball games and have races. Playing helps children learn skills they need as adults.

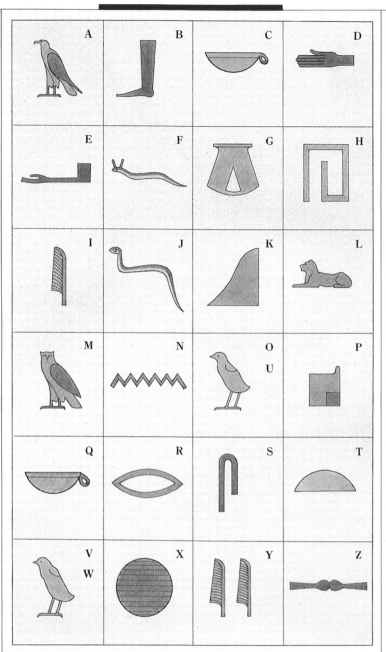

Egyptian writing

The symbols the Egyptians used for writing are called hieroglyphs. The Egyptians carved hieroglyphs on their temple walls and on the bases of statues. Scribes kept records written on papyrus.

For a long time the heiroglyphs' meaning was a mystery to archeologists. Then in 1821, Jean François Champollion deduced the meaning. There are more than 600 Egyptian hieroglyphs, and they often represent more than one thing. For example, the symbol for owl sometimes meant "owl" and sometimes meant the sound of "M," the first sound in the Egyptian word for owl.

Europeans have played the game of checkers since the 16th century. In the same century, the people of England began to play cricket, a game played with a ball and a bat. Baseball may have derived from this game.

Egyptians used these symbols at the end of a name to tell the reader whether the word referred to a man or a woman.

Renaissance people loved to play card games. These games took place in taverns and in private homes. Cribbage and whist, two popular Renaissance card games, are still played today.

Native American games Many plains tribes played "hoop and javelin," a game in which one person rolls a hoop across the ground and another tries to throw a spear through it. Points were given based on the accuracy of the throw.

Little girls living in castles played with rag dolls that had wax or wooden faces. Their brothers played war with wooden swords and held make-believe tournaments using straw men. During festivals children and adults played Hoodman's Bluff, a game similar to the modern Blindman's Bluff.

Music, song, and laughter echoed through the courts of the Middle Ages. Jugglers, minstrels, and bear trainers went from town to town entertaining the people.

A person born in the court of Louis XIV might have played with a kite or bow and arrow, or watched the ladies-in-waiting play chess and card games. Tennis was already a popular sport at this time. Tennis courts were indoors and had high cement walls. The ball could be played off the wall.

Native American sign language generally expresses ideas rather than words.

The sign for "eat" could mean "to eat" or "food," depending on the other signs used with it.

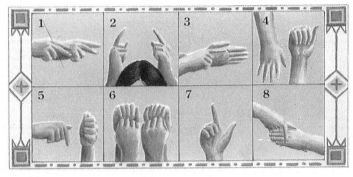

| 1. Dog | 2. Buffalo | 3. Can't | 4. Bad |
| 5. Bow | 6. Advice | 7. Moon | 8. Horse |

Native Americans used their hands, their movements, and even the way they painted their faces to communicate.

The names of Native American nations, animals, and objects can be communicated with sign language.

1. Hello 2. How many 3. Beaver 4. Friends

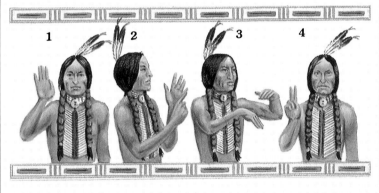

Often body movement accompanied the sign language. To say "How many?" the speaker stands in profile.

■ **Native Americans painted their faces in preparation for ceremonies and battle.** Face painting proclaimed their achievements.

The colors of paint used by Native Americans had different meanings for each tribe. The color red might represent life, while yellow symbolized the sun. For some, blue symbolized water and brown represented the earth.

Some Native Americans dressed in leather clothing decorated with porcupine quills, animal fur, beads, and horsehair. They wore their best clothing during ceremonies.

The native people of the Great Plains spoke many different languages. To understand each other, they invented a system of sign language that many settlers learned to understand. Early European traders also learned this sign language.

Some Native Americans also used smoke signals to communicate. Smoke signals' meanings varied from tribe to tribe.

■ Glossary

Acropolis: highest spot in a Greek city-state. The Greeks built their temples on the acropolis.

Andron: a room in an ancient Greek home used by men to entertain guests.

Archeology: the study of the way of life of those who lived before us. Archeologists dig in the earth to find artifacts (objects, weapons, bones, pottery, etc.).

Aristocracy: a privileged class of people who often have some control of the government.

Bishop: in the Catholic Church, a person who supervises several local churches.

Carbon: a nonmetallic element found in coal, charcoal, and diamonds. It is one of the ingredients in steel.

Cathedral: a church that contains the bishop's throne.

Citizen: in ancient Greece, a free person in a city-state.

Civilization: the culture and society of a certain group of people.

Colony: the settlement of a group of people, called colonists, who have left their country to live in another land but remain under the rule of their native country.

Customs: the habits of a group of people who live together.

Democracy: a political system by which the people choose the leaders of their government.

Descendants: the children, grandchildren, and great-grandchildren of a person.

Domesticate: to tame. Pigs, cows, sheep, and goats were once wild animals that people domesticated over the centuries. People first domesticated horses 4,000 years ago.

Facade: the front of a building which is usually decorated with sculpted details, columns, or painting.

Gladiator: a trained, Roman fighter who often fought to the death.

Guilds: in towns during the Middle Ages, artisans and crafts people banded together according to their craft into guilds.

Harpsichord: musical instrument with a keyboard, similar to an organ.

Homesteaders: people who were given ownership of land by living on it and cultivating it.

Legion: the Roman army was made up of legions comprised of foot soldiers (infantry) and soldiers on horseback (cavalry).

Literate: to be able to read and write.

Minting: to produce money. Roman emperors and the barbarian kings had their images pressed on coin pieces.

Palestra: a public place used by the ancient Greeks for sports training and exercise.

Papyrus: a plant found along the Nile whose stem was pressed to form paper; also the name of the paper formed from this plant.

Philosopher: someone who thinks about the large problems of the world.

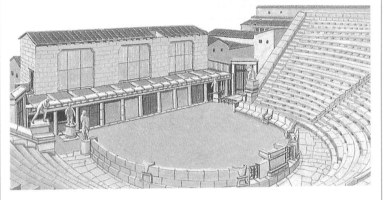

Reservations: areas of land set aside for Native Americans by the United States government when they were moved off their lands.

Sarcophagus: a stone coffin used by the ancient Egyptians. The body of the pharaoh was placed in the sarcophagus for burial.

Scurvy: a disease caused by a lack of vitamin C. Many early sailors suffered from this disease until they took citrus fruits along on their voyages.

Strigil: tool used by the ancient Greeks to scrape sweat and dirt from their bodies after sporting events.

Toga: a robe made from a single piece of fabric and worn by the Romans.

Tournament: a sport during the Middle Ages where soldiers would pretend to battle each other.

Tragedy: a sad or serious play. The opposite of a tragedy is the comedy, which makes us laugh.

Troubadour: a poet of the Middle Ages. Troubadours usually wrote poems and songs about love.

Vaccination: a medicine given to prevent diseases.

■ **Here is a list of museums you can visit to find out more about the evolution of culture. Check your local library for history museums or historic sites to visit in your area.**

American Museum of Natural History
Central Park West at 79th Street
New York, NY 10024
This is one of the world's largest natural history museums which features Native American and Inuit collections.

Museum of Civilization
Metcalf and McLeod Streets
Ottawa, Ontario
Canada K1A 0M8
This museum has an excellent collection of the arts and crafts of Inuit and Northwest Coast Native Americans.

Also check out Creative Education's Designing the Future series for the following books: *Cathedrals, Egyptian Pyramids, Mosques, Medieval Castles,* and *Greek Temples* and the It's a Fact! series for *Castles* and *Great Inventions.*

The Smithsonian
Washington, D.C.
http://www.si.du
The Smithsonian is comprised of several museums in the nation's capital. One history museum is the Smithsonian National Museum of American History.

University of Chicago
Oriental Institute Museum
1155 East 58th Street
Chicago, IL 60637
This museum's collections include archeology and art of ancient Babylonian, Egyptian, early Christian, and Islamic civilizations.

The entries in **bold** refer to whole chapters on the subject.